D1413294

Things That
No Longer
Delight Me

POETS
OUT LOUD

Series editor:
Elisabeth Frost

Things That
No Longer
Delight Me

Leslie C. Chang

poems

Fordham
University Press
New York
2010

Library of Congress Cataloging-in-Publication Data

Chang, Leslie (Leslie C.)
Things that no longer delight me : poems / Leslie Chang.—1st ed.
    p.   cm.— (Poets out loud.)
ISBN 978–0-8232–3199–7 (cloth : alk. paper)
ISBN 978–0-8232–3200–0 (pbk. : alk. paper)
I. Title.
PS3603.H35735T47   2010
811'.6—dc22

                                                    2009044883

Printed in the United States of America
12 11 10   5 4 3 2 1
First edition

for my family

Contents

Foreword

The poems in Leslie Chang's impressive first collection, *Things That No Longer Delight Me*, begin with a perfectly simple question, spoken presumably by the poet's grandmother, directed to both the poet and the reader: "Why are you interested in old stories?"

What struck me and won me over as a reader was the various ways Leslie Chang's poems respond to this question, with their quiet interweaving of past and present, of reclamation and loss, of histories whispered and revealed.

Sometimes, a first book of poems is a collection of rules and styles, hard learned and happily mastered. Other times, it's the greatest hits of the author's mentors, living or dead, a thankful tip of the hat before plunging into where their voice leads next.

Reading Leslie Chang's book made me think of the manuscript as lyric ark: a gathering up of all the vital elements that make up a world. It is a rich world, filled with dreads, desires, mysteries, photographs as Auguries, mulberries and hibiscus possible containers of restless spirits.

Here is an example to a departed relation in the poem "Errata":

> There is one refined portrait of you
> . . . .
> Even among your own children

your birthplace is a mystery. Buddhist
and poet, they say, spare with facts. . . .

Or a recipe in "Her Amah's Cure for Sties":

a scrap of silk   knot it round the knuckle
of a slender mulberry branch   bright bandage
sparrow banner   near hibiscus the wash drying

Or in the poem "Animism":

. . . Ahquen,
standing over a creel from the night market,
carves my grandfather's dying name, copying it
stroke by stroke onto the mosaic dome
of a live turtle's back. . . .

It's a world where the interior and exterior sometimes switch
places; other times can barely be told apart.

What is history, I thought as I read her manuscript, but the
stories we overhear? The first poem, where the grumpy grand-
mother asks the central question that powers this book, is enti-
tled "Salt," which I felt might be read two ways: The "salt" on
the family wounds by the poet's act of asking the questions
about the old stories, and the action of salt as a preservative,
that her poem in particular and her book in general save those
stories from the enemy of all poems: silence. Luckily for us,
the grandmother, mother, and aunts seem to have talked just
enough, and Leslie Chang's eyes and ears, music and nerve
were up to the challenge.

Here is Leslie Chang's wonderfully nuanced answer to probably the oldest question in the world. It's a beautifully lyric time machine.

Cornelius Eady
Associate Professor of English
The University of Notre Dame

Acknowledgments

Grateful acknowledgment is made to the editors of the following journals, where versions of these poems first appeared:

> *Agni*: "In the Language of the Here and Now, 4" and "In the Language of the Here and Now, 5"
> *The American Poetry Review*: "Things That No Longer Delight Me"
> *Barrow Street*: "Fragment (On Longing)"
> *Broadsided* (www.broadsidedpress.org): "Third Crescent Moon"
> *Crab Orchard Review*: "Shanghai, 1919, Redux"
> *Grolier Poetry Prize Annual, 2005*: "Aerogramme," "Errata," and "Salt"
> *The Iowa Review*: "Watermelons"
> *Literary Imagination*: "In the Language of the Here and Now, 1" (as "January") and "Montale's *You*"
> "Watermelons" was featured on the *Poetry Daily* Web site (www.poems.com).

To Cornelius Eady for selecting the book, my heartfelt thanks.

Thanks also to Elisabeth Frost and Helen Tartar for their guidance.

I wish to thank the Millay Colony for the Arts and the Bread Loaf Writers' Conference for generous gifts of time and community. I am also grateful to Wendy S. Walters for her gracious help with this book.

The form of "Things That No Longer Delight Me" was inspired by zuihitsu from Kimiko Hahn's *The Narrow Road to the Interior* (Norton, 2006) and *The Pillow Book of Sei Shōnagon*, translated and edited by Ivan Morris (Columbia University Press, 1991).

The title "Girl Resting on a Camel" is from The Metropolitan Museum of Art's exhibition, *China: Dawn of a Golden Age, 200–750 AD*.

"I Wish I Were a Brown Goose and Could Fly Back Home" is adapted from lines quoted by Susan Whitfield in *Life Along the Silk Road* (University of California Press, 1999). The title is from *Life Along the Silk Road*.

"To Lee Bontecou" is based on *A Conversation between Lee Bontecou and Mona Hadler*, The Graduate Center of the City University of New York, September 21, 2004.

Things That
No Longer
Delight Me

Salt

Why are you interested in old stories?
Mornings, my mother combed my hair.
She wept with me at the convent school.
I lost her to her father's intransigence.
My father, after a year-long absence,
to the charms of a girl barely older than I.
Our home, my siblings and I displaced
by a stepmother. The jackdaw in azalea
that bloomed red, luxuriant. The city
with its leafy enclaves. Then my country,
for good. My husband in the smoke
of incense I burnt, praying that he might
be taken from me. I never look back.

Errata

In fact, were you living, I could never
address you so casually or directly.
There is one refined portrait of you
with a small child seated on your lap:
you have a high forehead, and the sullen
girl slouching like her own cloth doll
is my grandmother, in whom you cultivated
an insatiable hunger when you disappeared
so early. Even among your own children
your birthplace is a mystery. Buddhist
and poet, they say, spare with facts. Also
that you were a high official's daughter
with classical learning. A minimalism I value
now that distance makes us intimates.

Her Amah's Cure for Sties

Little fort on the hillock   of the eyelid
a scrap of silk   knot it round the knuckle
of a slender mulberry branch   bright bandage
sparrow banner   near hibiscus the wash drying
and say three times a spell   whose words
have flown   trouble as small as a sesame seed
when she undid the silk   knot of forgetting
sun-blanched and frayed   by wind and rain
both the sty   and the node on the mulberry
through patient time healed   were gone

Aerogramme

The china blue of the window shade
   drawn afternoons against the sun. I first
encountered you in a letter Mother held
   in her hand—thin sheets of paper rarely
seen now, sky blue as if let in the window
   and crowded with what I know to be
your writing, minute characters in ballpoint
   impressing on anyone the cost
of being left behind and alone. I had almost
   forgotten you lived overseas when
I was still small. My little sister flew with
   Mother to see you. The cook and gardener
hid her in a hamper when it was time
   to leave. So many things recede and
fade like the colors and designs on stamps:
   a nearly weightless letter, its sender.

Watermelons

kept cold in the lake in net bags
    tied to emerald pleasure boats
        canopied and lit

by lanterns, on sweltering nights
    my mother and her cousins
        entertained themselves

playing cards, dancing and spitting
    the tear-shaped seeds overboard.
        Watermelons stored

under rosewood beds, Grandmother
    still remembers the summer
        retreat, its courtyards

planted with willows, wedding gifts
    spied in the banquet hall, one
        ripe melon cooling

in the well, like a recurring
    dream. And as if everything
        were foretold,

there are melon shapes, auspicious
    rows of windows, in the walled
        garden in Suzhou.

8

Shanghai, 1919

The three sisters wear black, ruffled bonnets.
The young men are languid in silk robes, straw
boaters. The sisters, hands folded, preside
in the frocks of their order, crêpe bows under
their chins. The pretty one has her hair parted,
her face is an oval. Impish, on the grass in a row
of eight sons by the first wife, my grandfather
on the right looks surprised. He must have known
his aunts by their skirts, an eclipse as they went
gliding past him. Then too much brightness.

Augury

I also know you in a ladylike cardigan
worn over a high-collared dress, arms crossed,
hairstyle clipped from the glossy pages
of 1950's *Vogue*, showing your widow's peak.
You pose with an unknown couple, the men
in soft-shouldered suits. Your sherbet-colored
sweaters Mother inherited at fifteen. A snapshot
I study the way a seer studies a sparrow's hollow
bones, like the heads you leave on a banquet plate
without apology, circulating among your guests.
How is it you are tight-lipped and I, soft-spoken.

Vanity

Hands clasped behind her back,
Grandmother walks, brisk
in black, cloth slippers, counting
under her breath. I've inherited

from her the habit of arriving
early, the smallness of her feet,
her discipline and her vanity.

Not her widow's peak, not
her luck at cards. Not her vigilance
against looking back, not the past.

Moon-gazing Chair

Last month Christie's sold another pair,
portable and antique as the actual stars.
An orchard party—the illustrated scene
from *Family*, the same chairs, matchstick-sized—
reproduced in the book-length catalogue.
Strange, what survives as art was ours—
low, elegant, gracing a household,
the pastime of a contemplation long lost.
Disassembled, explained the brief text,
each numbered joint fit in a cloth-lined box.
Memory and bone. Now this is the scene,
delicate and miniature under starlit boughs,
restoring what I know: you recited poems
in praise of—*white camellia, dowry*—the moon.

Augury Again

Tell me something about the future.
My mother's tortoiseshell combs
lie sideways in a drawer next to
her wristwatch and bamboo knitting
needles. This comes back now
with the indoor geranium's velvet
leaves: tired of waiting, an infant—
my brother!—crawled into a cardboard
box to sleep with a litter of kittens,
each one a ball of yarn. I've enough
longing to fill a Song dynasty tea-bowl
glazed a shiny brown and black, its
"hare's fur" pattern my own tulip mania—
predictable as the weather.

The Palmer Method

Foxing on the recipe copied in your hand,
    (from the palmers, those pilgrims returning
from a Holy Land, or our palms I read as
    a map with rivers, comparing life-lines?)
you did exercises to make your letters like
    the hoop a girl keeps rolling with a stick,
the girl in motion repeated also. I hear your
    Portuguese nun, her sibilants, the lights
kept low to cool the schoolroom in days of
    Dettol and flower water. Later you blew
smoke rings. Doodled in the method on
    a notepad, with Godmother on the telephone—
mornings the cord was pulled taut, extending out
    into the garden where you planted cosmos.
Each *O* a leaning portrait-oval, uniform as
    a child in a pleated skirt and knee socks.

Four Winds Dying Down

*I remember a woman who visited the house, carrying a small basket
like a sewing basket. She peddled jewelry for families needing money
during the war. The big, pearl ring your grandmother wears came
from her—she was called Bing Zu. She claimed that ring had been
retrieved from a grave. Bing Zu appeared at our door one morning,
pale. "Did you find a small basket?" she asked your grandmother
who laughed, "What basket?" before returning it to her.*

Wonder in her voice, my mother
is a child, alert and disinterested,
watching her mother with the visitor

in the sunken living room,
its lemon-colored sofa and pearwood
drumstools on Stubbs Road,

halfway up the Peak,
a view of junks bobbing like toys
on the harbor. Once she went

downstairs to breakfast to find
a mahjong party still in progress:
jade brooches fastened to evening dress,

each glimmering like a morning star.
Half-remembered, as if half-witnessed,
the game's four winds dying down.

Now the visitor reappears
on the threshold, sighing her relief
at finding the tidy bamboo or rush

basket with butterfly hinges.
As if its hidden contents—rustle of tissue
my mother still hears—were good fortune,

passing from one set of hands to another,
and the basket—the past remembered
lightly is the only way to bear it—fate.

Solitaire

Smoke-colored, misshapen, diamond-set,
the outsized pearl on your finger shimmers
in broad daylight as you turn over cards
from a deck you hold in one hand, never
one to be summoned. You sit at your desk
under an aquatint of a Tahitian woman
and a framed letter, your mother's calligraphy
in neat columns, the playing cards laid out
as if they tell the future. Half a century gone by,
and countless games of solitaire you played
since your husband's death—to pass the time.
You linger here, hearts and spades like notes
in a thrush's song, unbitter in a New World.

The Entrance Exam

Hong Kong, 1950

Ahquen tells her to hurry, without herself knowing
what for.

Garden Road where one waited for the tram to the Peak;
flowers like wild birds tamed by placards in the botanical gardens;

An acacia in a gravel courtyard, two stone staircases
lead to a classroom full of children.

the smell of burnt sugar, street vendors stirred chestnuts
in demerara and sand.

A girl with everything in threes—brush, ruler, gum eraser—
lends my mother what she needs.

I can see her face clearly.

Weeks later, a houseguest reading the morning paper discovers
my mother's name on its front page, in a sea
of matriculated students' names.

A white blouse bought in Kowloon, the emblem
on its left pocket, Our Lady blue.

The Star Ferry, streamlined and fast, in the harbor
of things I remember.

Shanghai, 1919, Redux

It is summer, late
morning birdsong quelled by heat.
My great-aunts, three sisters

stationed among relatives
in the ornate garden, there are shadows
before a rainstorm.

A missing detail, spoken
offhandedly, revises what I know,
Theirs was an order for widows.

The oldest ran off, took vows
when she learned that a marriage
was arranged for her. Her sisters

followed. So this story
has to do with deciding one's own fate,
and the bond between sisters,

unless, bereft of a future,
my aunt with her oval-shaped face
was in love with someone else.

Which rearranges the visible,
marring their otherworldly stillness
held for the tented camera:

ruffled bonnets, black silk dresses.
A widow-bird opens its wing, and the rest
is hearsay, conjecture pure.

Animism

A water-jar guards the concrete step.
Beyond the open kitchen door, Ahquen,
standing over a creel from the night market,
carves my grandfather's dying name, copying it
stroke by stroke onto the mosaic dome
of a live turtle's back, moss and more turtles
wriggling at her feet. Now, like smoke, thread
trails from a needle stuck in the candle-end
you recycled as a pincushion, nothing wasted.
Panic-stricken, you once went with her to burn
incense at the Buddhist temple, succumbing
to custom. I know better than to ask again how
it was done: the story goes she was sorrowful
enough to set them free, carry them to the river.

I amass details,

        jade bracelet, her animal-print

dresses, an oval coral cameo

Things That No Longer Delight Me

After Sei Shōnagon

genealogy

We're talking about genealogy, my grand-uncle says, gathered with his siblings in near darkness at the foot of my grandmother's hospital bed.

osmanthus

Or sweet olive. Its fragrant white flowers. My mother makes dumplings filled with black sesame paste, boiling them in sugar water perfumed with the dried flowers, which float in the bowl like tired stars. A ceramic spoon.

When I visited my great-grandfather's youngest sister she offered me a bowl of these dumplings—something sweet for a child. She also gave me a letter written by my great-grandmother. It closes with a poem in the classical style, describing the brilliance of autumn and alluding to her own illness.

letters written in autumn

family snapshots

the weeping inkstone

tricks of light

powder puffs made from swan's down

the web of family

ancestral homes

I bought a cheap, woodblock print in Suzhou, my
grandmother's birthplace, charmed by its piney grays and
greens. Bright umbrellas float over the bridges.

On our way to the Stone Lion Garden, she and I watched
visitors paddle colorful boats as rain fell on the miniature
canals. That night at the restaurant I listened to her ordering
the dishes. She spoke in the local dialect, playing up its coy
sibilants. The persistence with which those *s* sounds swim in
my ear.

my mother's pet silkworms

As a child my mother collected mulberry leaves to feed them.
Traveling together in China, we looked for a mulberry tree. She
pointed to a shrub with pink flowers like pompons.

persimmons

I will always be fascinated by details from my grandmother's
childhood. She told me once that she had to walk a long way to
her first school, in Hong Kong, and I imagine a tiny version of
her, memory like a set of painted, nesting dolls. Undergoing
radiation treatment, taking a taxi alone to the hospital on a daily
basis—past the supermarket called Mollie Stone's, through
Laurel Heights—she said it was like going to school.

bronze mirrors

chrysanthemums

a moon gate

The Flower Market

I can't find you in the crowd. Women stroll, arm in arm, the busy streets strewn with petals like confetti and red firecracker paper. They carry home quince branches in the smoke-filled air. An auntie savors rock candy. The mouth of a household god is filled with money. You must be here. Where the outgoing year meets a new one in so many jostling bodies, your absence begins to feel willful. Just last year, you described the festival to me, relishing the human drama. I can't find you in the world.

camphor

colophons

San Francisco Bay

her iron scissors

night-blooming jasmine

mosquito coils

the Stone Lion Garden

a zigzag pattern called "cracked-ice"

the chestnut cake she loved

a painting of grooms and horses

a magpie in a patch of tawny sky

her sewing box

Burma

talking snapdragons

Horse Horse Tiger Tiger

You are standing   near me
present when I   prepare breakfast
wash the dishes   fold laundry
mince scallions   make egg soup
saying *how can you   do it like that*
your voice amused   disapproving
there's a right way   and a wrong way
to do things   you showed me how
making the bed   together we
smoothed the sheets   arranged
a mohair blanket   at the foot
anything in-between   is senseless:
horse   horse   tiger   tiger
not one thing   or another

Serindia

People's Square

The heart of the exercise is in moving
slow. Slow windmills with hands and feet,
nothing more vigorous

than this shadow-boxing
to an eccentric tempo. As if slow
were a color: scarves waved and thrown

by old-timers practicing
to a loudspeaker. I want to move
that slow, re-learning Strauss waltzes,

bundled against the cold—slow
as the smile on the man pedaling
a bicycle-cart to move a mountain of coal.

Shaanxi Province

There are tall persimmon trees
with coppery branches like beacon fires
and pomegranate orchards keeping
the terraced landscape in place.

The foothills slope, coming and going,
and a small outpost above the river
lets fall its leaves in surrender,
an elaborate tribal banner.

Gansu Province

Farmer and ox plow beneath rain clouds
on a cave wall. In Gansu Province,
a woman winnowing, chaff

falls from the air like golden rain.
A man uses a switch on his stubborn mare,
and women carry knitting in their baskets.

The saw-toothed mountains are identical
to blue-green, stylized ones a pilgrim progresses
through, zigzagging on a cave wall,

so that I see myself in the unpainted places.
A giant, red sun hovers over the province
as farmer and ox plow beyond dust clouds.

Urumqi

You say your country is the shape
of a rooster. Your province is near the tail.
Baby camels in a wild herd stumble
over the scrubby face of a dune. Your father
is a retired official, your mother one of many sisters.
Your son drinks a glass of milk for breakfast,
five apricots in it, like winter suns.

Girl Resting on a Camel

Desert brightness and distance
like the white, earthenware body
of a Tang camel, a girl resting on top.

Wearing a tunic over pants
and high, soft boots, riding
between two shaggy humps

in the valley of a dream,
she sees her parents' house
where apricots litter the orchard.

Sure-footed, her camel
carries her weightless soul,
accustomed to the glare

and gravel emptiness it takes
to arrive anywhere. An eternity.

The Parable of the Conjured Land

I was in a landscape,
a story told over and over.
In the shadow of a minaret, I stood watching
as men buried grapevines for the winter.

Under a brilliant sky, cloudless and birdless,
the upper reaches of the atmosphere windswept.
Yellow poplars surrounding the arbor. In the distance,
a flock of fuzzy sheep grazed on tired upland.

We had crossed dusty, wide avenues
to arrive. Donkey carts and motorcycles
crowded arcades trellised with flourishing vines.
A mirror hung from the lowest branch of a tree
at one crossroads, trapping the sunlight.

I Wish I Were a Brown Goose and Could Fly Back Home

Having left my father's court,
I live in the nomads' camp. I wear fur and felt,
my robes scented with musk and rosewater
and folded for the long journey by a tearful maid
useless now. The water is brackish.
Even tea tastes salt, boiled with mutton fat—
I can hardly swallow it.
I was traded for the flying horses.
They graze in hidden pastures above the river.

I am learning songs on a barbarian flute.

Goldenrod—the peaked cap

        a court official wears, bowing

Montale's *You*

But we can love a shade, you know,
being shades ourselves.
Xenia I

We could see a bridge mirrored as a wheel.
I thumb through the pages of your datebook,
Montale, looking for my name in Waterman ink—
Saturday, Sunday, Monday, that hat trick.
On the station platform, I read
the departures board, a student of orthography.
The shuffling destinations, a noisy wasp,
apse, rhapsody—I mishear your *rasp*. Then you
gaze beyond the frame with unsettling stillness.
My great-grandfather, a young man, wears
a scholar's robes with a tweed hunting cap.
I also look for my others in smoke.
In the gingko leaf, a courtesan's tiny fan.
Like the customs official, visitations never troubled you.
You knew how to receive a guest. With a gift.

Bright Earth

The double-jointed aunt,
the card-shark, and the aunt
who was good at jacks; my mother's
cousin who told ghost stories, the devout
aunts who went to Mass everyday, and
the one whose hands smelled of anise.

The aunt who raised orchids,
the amateur herbalist—her remedy
for canker sores, I can still taste
it on the tip of my tongue, that bitter,
orange powder. The seamstress,

the ballroom-dancing champion,
the concert pianist, and the aunt who
was first in her class—glimpsed beyond
an octagonal doorframe in the women's library,
where surely she studied *The Analects*.

Fragment (On Longing)

What if I didn't know her to be the moon's namesake,
a harvest moon low in the sky when she was born, the salted
                                                        yolk
in each mooncake recalling that brightness and closeness,
                                        calling her back.

Third Crescent Moon

After Ritsos

Whenever I think of crab, my aunt sighs, I think of your grandmother. Steam rises from a dented pot. Live crabs wrestle in the sink. Being careful not to cut my knuckles with the cleaver, slicing ginger into slivers for shallow dishes of black vinegar, I think that I am just like my aunt, who remembers then forgets. Her memory failing. Grief enters the kitchen like a Tang noblewoman on horseback, wearing a tiny balaclava. She rides her diminutive piebald side-saddle. Dust covers the lindens, which are in bloom again.

In the Language of the Here and Now

I

After a mid-winter death, I heard my aunts
say, *He couldn't pass through that gate.*

You are like a Silk Route merchant with
a caravan, in their old idiom; or a minor
official sent to the border regions

to collect a salt tax. Every city has a gate,
the narrow portal between seasons. Difficult to pass.

In unaccustomed light, the daily banishment
of what you knew before, bitter flavors, foreign cold.

Come spring, showers harrow the road,
its shoulder the muted color of an astrakhan coat,
iris in long grass circling weathered milestones.

Forbearance in their words for one arriving
at a new city, seeing the tall embankment, wanting rest.

2

Nearing Xi'an, one sees the grassy swell
of unexcavated mounds.

Jewelweed grows in the ancient wall.
Beyond an archway the dusty thoroughfare
is an axis laid down

at the center of the world, where merchants
once traded in glass beads

and silk like gold. I look for you in
children's faces. And in the provincial museum,

its underground galleries.
Shadowy, behind glass, small sculptures:
a serving girl and a lion-colored mongrel.

In a side room, a carriage painted black
with swirling clouds that signify an afterlife.

3

An ocher camel, bit in its open mouth,
kneels in the dusty, ill-lit museum case.

In Han and Tang dynasties,
the dead were buried with funerary sculptures,
reminders of the here and now.

Miniature, animated like this
retinue of servants carrying everyday things,

figurines once lined potters' shelves:
commonplace, earthenware, numberless.

Here and now, I am attendant
or dromedary, bearing a dowager's worldly
goods in a province remote as an afterlife.

You braved sandstorms to reach an orchard,
leading a camel glazed with the steppe's mineral shades.

4

My mother and my grandmother returning
to China are ravenous, as if poised

on a threshold: October markets
glimpsed from the taxi entice them,
stalls with melons and persimmons, a Kodachrome

from childhood. They request
to stop at the stand selling hot milk in wooden bowls.

My grandmother sniffs air thick with coal smoke
for the scent of burnt sugar; she will follow her nose
into a labyrinthine *hutong*, forsaking us.

For my mother, it's the dried watermelon seeds
she used to crack and eat compulsively, leaving a trail

in a dark wood. But nothing they buy on our way back
from the Temple of Heaven tastes as they remember it.

5

At the mouth of a lane snaking beyond
the concourse, a river of bicycles swallowed me.

I was lost among crowded stalls, the air
bruised with coal smoke, at some border between
despair and wanting to be lost.

I hadn't yet eaten the seeds that would
keep me there, though the place

was what I hungered for: a forgotten past,
the same iron weights and measures,

old men in a willow's filigreed shade
playing dominoes, their companions finches
and canaries in bamboo cages, tiny souls

flickering like taillights on the bicycles
I followed. To be led back out in amazement.

6

The voice on the recorded tour
guides me in English from a dusty vestibule

into the first of many courtyards,
serpents and birds perched on the eaves
of yellow-tiled roofs to ward off spirits.

Imperial yellow, heavenly, the rooftops
multiply above inner courtyards.

In each of my forbidden cities there
is something that once belonged to you.

Biscuit-tins, my host that night
at dinner confides, were discovered in
the palace storerooms, unopened for a century.

Listening, I see immense shadows from a lantern
held by a palace guard, running past with news of a theft.

7

You are also like a country fortified by a wall.
At the Great Wall, we ride the funicular

to an eastern gatehouse, and from that height
we can see other sections of the wall
winding through the hills

like a dragon,
the same burnished landscape on either side.

We climb steps
dating from the Warring States period,

to where a girl sells felt tigers.
I buy one with a double aspect—crimson
on one side, burnt orange on the other.

Returning to Beijing, old trucks trundle past,
the road lined with poplars like an ancient army.

8

Now no one guards the tomb
except for the man in carpet slippers,

selling tickets from a paper wheel.
His comrades playing *go* mind a grandchild.

I enter the empty tomb of a Han princess
buried with slaves while still in her girlhood,
waist-high lilies and a door painted on the walls.

I chose you as my guide, knowing
little of you, not much more than your intense gaze:

that you learned to drive on the Corniche,
that you broadcast sonatas on the midnight radio.

You remain as broken to me as the terracotta
soldier a farmer stumbled over, plowing his field—
his find startling blackbirds feeding there like shades.

To Lee Bontecou

In memory of my grandmother, Cecilia Shen
(1915–2005)

I

I keep a photograph of your studio

nearby,

its unfinished shelves

reminding me what's necessary.

Reminding me

that I'm like-minded: I like objects for company,

to decorate the plainest spaces, decorum.

Studies,

hybrid forms from nature,

what collects there:

a zebra-striped teapot,

another with the delicate brown and white

markings of a nautilus or some animal

that grazes,

an example of Yixing stoneware.

There are patterned shapes like

                                    an urchin's,

a small opening where the animal made its exit,

and blue spherical orbs—

                              a lonely eye

or a battered planet, stopped in its tracks.

2

Stilled. As if, without a center of gravity,

                                        it lost

its way, its orbit lost, thrown by grief from a system.

I amass details,

                        jade bracelet, her animal-print

dresses, an oval coral cameo, and the silver,

lamé shoes, like sparkly fish.

                              A little bit of time,

and you can solve all your problems,

I've heard you say. Winter evenings in your barn studio,

                                            listening

in the gloom to the radio's drone, you

tinkered with models from your brother's youth:

piecing balsa

       with rice-paper,

you made submarines and skipjacks.

                 The sleek hulls

and masts grew into ethereal fins.

From your compulsion.

         Here I am,

addressing another *you*.

3

I collect postcards, a small reproduction

               in color

of a luminous fish: its amber and orange markings.

Postcard of a barn,

         stranded in this field of light.

Amber and ocher on all sides.

Inside its belly, the rough-hewn walls resemble your studio's.

My window overlooks a meadow

           the barn overshadows.

All season, I've collected names for things

                                         I'll lose:

monarch in loosestrife, dragonfly like a biplane.

Goldenrod—the peaked cap

                             a court official wears, bowing,

yellow denoting earth and east in the old cosmology.

The russet

                 apples hold onto the ornate branches and refuse

to fall. A blue jay

speaks to me of sudden joy. Heaven,

                                 the ancients wrote,

lay just beyond the western mountains.